Dear Parents and Educators,

Welcome to Penguin Young Readers! As parents and educators, you know that each child develops at his or her own pace—in terms of speech, critical thinking, and, of course, reading. Penguin Young Readers recognizes this fact. As a result, each Penguin Young Readers book is assigned a traditional easy-to-read level (1–4) as well as a Guided Reading Level (A–P). Both of these systems will help you choose the right book for your child. Please refer to the back of each book for specific leveling information. Penguin Young Readers features esteemed authors and illustrators, stories about favorite characters, fascinating nonfiction, and more!

Slow, Slow Sloths

LEVEL **2**

GUIDED READING LEVEL **I**

This book is perfect for a **Progressing Reader** who:
- can figure out unknown words by using picture and context clues;
- can recognize beginning, middle, and ending sounds;
- can make and confirm predictions about what will happen in the text; and
- can distinguish between fiction and nonfiction.

Here are some **activities** you can do during and after reading this book:
- Nonfiction: Nonfiction books deal with facts and events that are real. Talk about the elements of nonfiction. Discuss some of the facts you learned about sloths.
- Sight Words: Sight words are frequently used words that readers know just by looking at them. They are known instantly, on sight. Knowing these words helps children develop into efficient readers. As you read the story, have the child point out the sight words below.

are	has	no	round	there
as	live	of	take	they

Remember, sharing the love of reading with a child is the best gift you can give!

—Bonnie Bader, EdM
 Penguin Young Readers program

*Penguin Young Readers are leveled by independent reviewers applying the standards developed by Irene Fountas and Gay Su Pinnell in *Matching Books to Readers: Using Leveled Books in Guided Reading*, Heinemann, 1999.

For David—slow, but steady!—BB

PENGUIN YOUNG READERS
An Imprint of Penguin Random House LLC

Photo credits: cover: (baby sloth) © Thinkstock/Snic320,(climbing sloth) © Thinkstock/Eric Isselée; page 3, 15: © Getty Images/Hoberman Collection; page 4: © Thinkstock/JonathanNicholls; page 5: © Thinkstock/SivelstreSelva; pages 6–7: © Thinkstock/Eric Isselée; page 8: © Thinkstock/ctrlaplus1; page 9: © Thinkstock/miroslav_1; page 10: © Thinkstock/Julio Viard; page 11: © Thinkstock/JackF; page 12: © Thinkstock/Eric Isselée; page 13: © Thinkstock/webguzs; page 14: © Thinkstock/JackKa; page 16: © Thinkstock/Jozev; page 17: © Getty Images/Wolfgang Kaehler; page 18: © Getty Images/Hoberman Collection; page 19: © Corbis; page 20: © Thinkstock/ Eric Middelkoop; page 21: © Getty Images/DEA /C. DANI I. JESKE; pages 22–23: © Thinkstock/Seubsai; page 24: (ants) © Thinkstock/onlyyouqj, (grasshopper) © Thinkstock/Andreas Argirakis, (lizard) © Thinkstock/ananaline, (mosquito) © Thinkstock/JoyTasa; page 25: © Corbis/Suzi Eszterhas; page 26: © Getty Images/RODRIGO ARANGUA; page 27: © Corbis/Piotr Naskrecki; page 28: © Corbis/ James Christensen; page 29: © Corbis/Wayne Lynch; page 30: © Getty Images/RODRIGO ARANGUA; page 31: © Thinkstock/Adam_C_King; page 32: © Thinkstock/tane-mahuta.

Text copyright © 2016 by Bonnie Bader. All rights reserved. Published by Penguin Young Readers, an imprint of Penguin Random House LLC, 345 Hudson Street, New York, New York 10014. Manufactured in China.

Library of Congress Cataloging-in-Publication Data is available.

ISBN 978-0-399-54116-2 (pbk)   ·   10 9 8 7 6 5 4 3 2 1
ISBN 978-0-399-54117-9 (hc)   10 9 8 7 6 5 4 3 2 1

SLOW, SLOW SLOTHS

by Bonnie Bader

Penguin Young Readers
An Imprint of Penguin Random House

Slow,

slow

sloths!

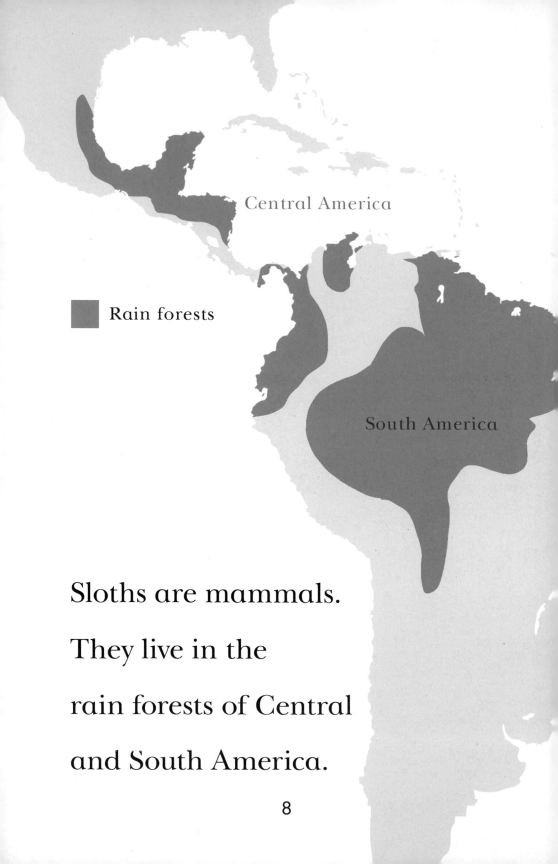

Central America

Rain forests

South America

Sloths are mammals.
They live in the
rain forests of Central
and South America.

8

Sloths have long arms
and long fur.
Are they in the
same family
as monkeys?

No!

Sloths are in the same family

as armadillos.

And anteaters.

There are two types of sloths.

The two-toed sloth has two claws

on its front feet.

The three-toed sloth
has three claws on its
front feet.

All sloths have round heads.

And three- to four-inch claws.

And little ears.

And short tails.

And sad-looking eyes.

15

But the three-toed sloth

looks like it is always smiling!

Sloths are born high up

in the trees.

Baby sloths cling to

their mothers' bellies

until they can take care

of themselves.

A young sloth likes to stay close

to its mother.

It can live with her

for up to four years.

Now it is all grown up.

It is about two feet long.

It weighs between 8 and 17 pounds.

Sloths like to live
by themselves.

They sleep a lot.
Sloths sleep between
15 and 20 hours a day.

Two-toed sloths
are awake at night.

Sloths hook their claws onto
tree branches.
They hang upside down
by their long arms.

Sloths sleep and sleep and sleep.

23

Sloths don't eat much.

They sometimes eat small insects.

Or small lizards.

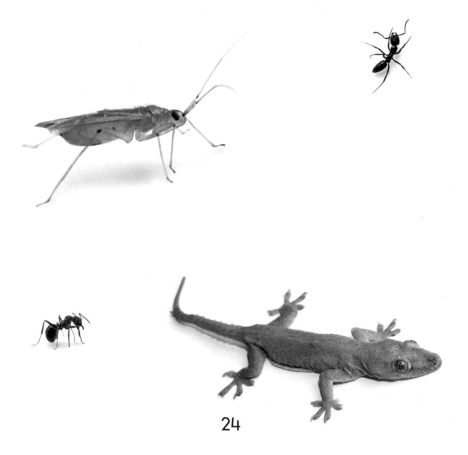

But they mostly eat leaves.

Leaves do not give them
much energy.

This is one reason sloths are
so slow!

The sloth's long claws make it hard to walk on the ground. So it stays in the trees.